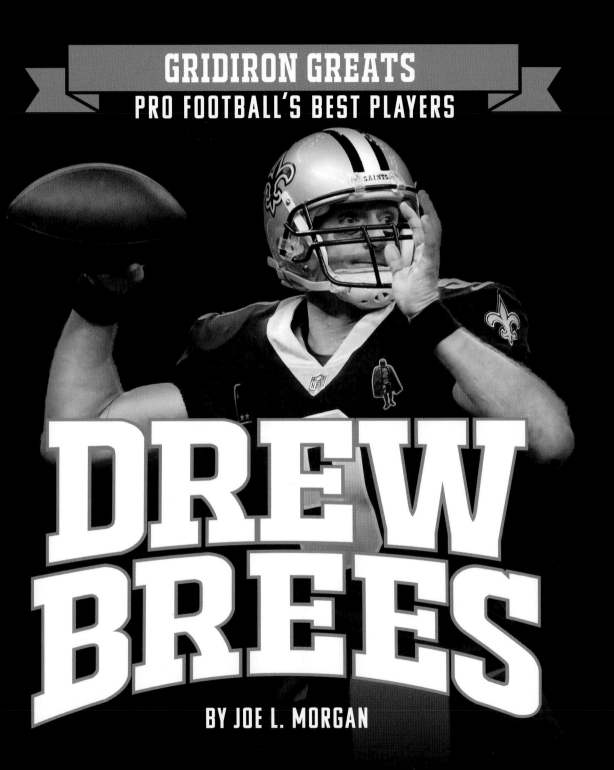

GRIDIRON GREATS
PRO FOOTBALL'S BEST PLAYERS

DREW BREES

BY JOE L. MORGAN

GRIDIRON GREATS
PRO FOOTBALL'S BEST PLAYERS

AARON RODGERS

ANTONIO BROWN

DREW BREES

J.J. WATT

JULIO JONES

ROB GRONKOWSKI

RUSSELL WILSON

TOM BRADY

VON MILLER

GRIDIRON GREATS
PRO FOOTBALL'S BEST PLAYERS

DREW BREES

BY JOE L. MORGAN

MASON CREST

Mason Crest
450 Parkway Drive, Suite D
Broomall, Pennsylvania 19008
(866) MCP-BOOK (toll-free)
www.masoncrest.com

First printing
9 8 7 6 5 4 3 2 1

ISBN (hardback) 978-1-4222-4198-1
ISBN (series) 978-1-4222-4067-0
ISBN (ebook) 978-1-4222-7610-5

Cataloging-in-Publication Data on file with the Library of Congress

NATIONAL
HIGHLIGHTS

Developed and Produced by National Highlights Inc.
Editor: Andrew Luke
Interior and cover design: Jana Rade, impact studios
Production: Michelle Luke

QR CODES AND LINKS TO THIRD-PARTY CONTENT

CONTENTS

KEY ICONS TO LOOK FOR:

 Words to Understand: These words with their easy-to-understand definitions will increase the reader's understanding of the text while building vocabulary skills.

 Sidebars: This boxed material within the main text allows readers to build knowledge, gain insights, explore possibilities, and broaden their perspectives by weaving together additional information to provide realistic and holistic perspectives.

 Educational Videos: Readers can view videos by scanning our QR codes, providing them with additional educational content to supplement the text. Examples include news coverage, moments in history, speeches, iconic sports moments and much more!

 Text-Dependent Questions: These questions send the reader back to the text for more careful attention to the evidence presented there.

 Research Projects: Readers are pointed toward areas of further inquiry connected to each chapter. Suggestions are provided for projects that encourage deeper research and analysis.

 Series Glossary of Key Terms: This back-of-the book glossary contains terminology used throughout this series. Words found here increase the reader's ability to read and comprehend higher-level books and articles in this field.

WORDS TO UNDERSTAND

DRAMATIC – sudden and extreme

FEAT – an act or product of skill, endurance, or ingenuity

FINALE – the close or termination of something: such as the last and often climactic event or item in a sequence

OVERTIME – the extra period of play in a contest

REGULATION – the standard period of time established by the rules of a game or contest

CHAPTER 1

GREATEST MOMENTS

DREW BREES' NFL CAREER

From early on, it was apparent that Drew Brees was destined to become a great NFL quarterback. Brees played high school football in Austin, TX, at Westlake ("Chaparrals") High School, winning a state championship and MVP honors in his senior year. He was recruited to play quarterback at Purdue University of the Big Ten Conference in West Lafayette, IN, where he won both athletic and academic honors. He graduated from Purdue in 2001 with a degree in Industrial Management.

Brees entered the 2001 NFL Draft after having a successful college career at Purdue. The San Diego (now Los Angeles) Chargers selected him with the 32nd pick. Brees took over for an injured Doug Flutie to become the Chargers starting QB, only to suffer a shoulder injury at the end of 2005. He took an offer to play for New Orleans beginning in the 2006 season, leaving the Chargers in the hands of another rising gridiron star, Philip Rivers.

Since his draft selection, Brees has started 249 games in seventeen NFL seasons for the Chargers and Saints. He has been honored with several awards, including Offensive Player of the Year twice. The winning QB of Super Bowl XLIV, Brees is on his way to earning one more honor at the end of his playing career: induction to the Pro Football Hall of Fame in Canton, OH.

DREW BREES CAREER HIGHLIGHTS

Brees has established himself as a gridiron great of the NFL. He was named a first-team All-Pro in the 2006 season, where he led the Saints to a 10–6 record, three years before winning Super Bowl XLIV. He has also been named to eleven Pro Bowls in his seventeen-year NFL career and has earned two NFL AP Offensive Player of the Year awards. Here's a summary of his important statistics at quarterback:

- 70,445 passing yards for his career. Drew Brees is the third quarterback in NFL history to pass for 70,000 yards or more in his career.
- NFL record 471 pass completions in 2016, 1st all-time for a single season. Brees broke his own record of 468 pass completions set in 2011.
- 5,476 passing yards in 2011 NFL season (2nd all-time). Brees is one of five players to pass for 5,000+ yards in a season (Matthew Stafford, Dan Marino, Tom Brady, and Peyton Manning) and is the only NFL quarterback with multiple 5,000-yard seasons (five).
- 96.7% career passer rating. Brees has a career passing rating that is 6th all-time for NFL QBs.

The San Diego Chargers initially drafted Brees, and he played there for his first five NFL seasons (2001–2005) before establishing himself among the NFL's elite quarterbacks as the leader of the New Orleans Saints.

BREES' GREATEST CAREER MOMENTS

HERE IS A LIST OF SOME OF THE CAREER FIRSTS AND GREATEST ACHIEVEMENTS BY DREW BREES DURING HIS TIME IN THE NFL TO DATE.

FIRST PLAYOFF TOUCHDOWN PASS (2005)

The 2004 NFL season was a special one for Drew Brees. After coming off a disappointing 2–9 record in 2003 that saw him benched for veteran Doug Flutie and the team taking Philip Rivers in the 2004 NFL Draft, Brees led the San Diego Chargers to an 11–4 record (the team finished the season 12–4 as Brees sat out the final game of the season). The effort was good enough to lead the Chargers back to the playoffs and NFL Comeback Player of the Year honors for Brees, along with an AFC Pro Bowl selection. In a January 8, 2005, home matchup against the NY Jets, Brees kept the Chargers competitive, throwing his first playoff touchdown pass. He would finish the game 31–42 passing for 319 yards and two touchdowns, including a drive that tied the game in the 4th quarter at 17 points, before losing in overtime to the Jets by the score 20–17.

Brees completes a 26-yard pass to WR Keenan McCardell in the left corner of the end zone for his first career playoff touchdown pass. [Begin at the 0:44 second mark in the video]

FIRST SUPER BOWL VICTORY (XLIV)

Brees made his first Super Bowl appearance in Super Bowl XLIV, on February 7, 2010, in a matchup against AFC Champions Indianapolis Colts in Miami's Hard Rock Stadium. The game was a matchup between two of the game's premier quarterbacks, Brees and the Colts' Peyton Manning. Down 10–6 at halftime, Brees led the Saints back in the second half, finishing the game with 32 pass completions, an 82 percent pass-completion rate, two touchdowns, and 288 yards passing. The Saints defeated the Colts 31–17 and Brees was named the game's MVP.

Video highlights of Drew Brees Super Bowl XLIV MVP performance against the Indianapolis Colts, on February 7, 2010.

FIFTH NFL QB TO REACH 50,000 YARDS

Drew Brees entered a December 8, 2013, game against the Carolina Panthers nee
287 yards to reach the 50,000-yard career passing mark. A 15-yard 2nd-quarter pa
TE Josh Hill put Brees over the top. Brees finished the game with 313 yards passing
four touchdowns on 30–42 passing (71.4 percent completion rate) as the Saints bea
Panthers by the score of 31–13. The effort made Brees the fifth quarterback in NFL hi
to pass for 50,000 yards; nine quarterbacks after the 2017 season have reached 50,000
passing (including
Brees): Marino, Brett
Favre, Peyton and Eli
Manning, Ben Roeth-
isberger, Philip Rivers,
John Elway, and Tom
Brady.

TE Josh Hill rumbles 15 yards on a pass reception from Drew Brees in the 2nd quarter of a December 28, 2013, game against the Carolina Panthers. The catch made Brees the fifth QB in NFL history to go over 50,000 yards for a career.

THIRD NFL QB TO REACH 70,000 YARDS

Near the end of the 2017 season, Brees came into a game against rival Atlanta on December 24, 2017, with the possibility of surpassing 70,000 passing yards in his NFL career. Brees passed the milestone after a 1st-quarter pass to his running back Mark Ingram and finished the game (a 23–13 victory) 21–28 passing for 239 yards, a touchdown and an interception. Brees went on to finish the 2017 season with 70,445 yards passing for his NFL career. Only Peyton Manning (71,940) and Brett Favre (71,838) have more career passing yards than Brees, but given his season average of 4,144 yards over the past seventeen NFL seasons, he should set a new league record of nearly 75,000 yards at the end of the 2018 season.

Drew Brees completes a 12-yard screen pass to RB Mark Ingram in the first quarter of a game against the Atlanta Falcons, on December 24, 2017.

MOST PASS COMPLETIONS IN AN NFL SEASON (2016)

Drew Brees has proven himself to be one of the best passers in the history of the NFL. During a January 1, 2017 game against the Atlanta Falcons, a team that Brees seems to set a lot of records or reach milestones against, Brees hit running back Travaris Cadet with a 3-yard pass in the 4th quarter of a 38–32 loss. The completion, with 45 seconds left in the game, gave Brees a career single-season record of 471 completions, surpassing his own record of 468 yards that he set in 2011. In fact, Brees holds six of the top ten single-season totals for passing completions, including the top three positions.

In a January 1, 2017, regular season **finale** against the Atlanta Falcons, Drew Brees completes his record-setting 471st pass for the season, a 3-yard, 4th-quarter pass to RB Travaris Cadet.

250 TOUCHDOWNS IN HIS NFL CAREER

At the 5:34 mark of the 1st quarter in an October 23, 2011, game against the Indianapolis Colts, Brees threw a 4-yard score to WR Marques Colston for his 250th career NFL touchdown. It was his second of 5 touchdown passes in the game. The throw and catch made Drew Brees one of only twenty-one quarterbacks in NFL history to throw at least 250 touchdowns in a career.

Watch Brees hit favorite target Marques Colston for TD pass number 250 of his career.

FIFTH QB TO THROW 400 TOUCHDOWNS IN HIS NFL CAREER

Drew Brees reached 400 touchdown passes in his NFL career in **dramatic** fashion. Playing to a 20–20 tie in **regulation** time, the Saints won the toss to begin **overtime** in an October 4, 2015, game against the Dallas Cowboys. Brees' first pass attempt in overtime was incomplete; he came back with an 80-yard pass completion to RB C.J. Spiller to win the game 26–20. The touchdown throw was Brees' 400th career touchdown pass. He is tied with Tom Brady for the third-most touchdowns thrown (488) in a career and joins Dan Marino (420), Brett Favre (508), and Peyton Manning (539) as the only quarterbacks with at least 400 in a career.

Brees, on the second play of an overtime game against the Dallas Cowboys, October 4, 2015, completes an 80-yard pass to RB C.J. Spiller, good for the game winning touchdown and the 400th touchdown pass for Brees.

MOST SEASONS WITH 5,000+ PASSING YARDS (5)

Brees has averaged more than 4,000 yards passing a season for his seventeen-year NFL career. He is the only quarterback to pass for 5,000 yards in more than one season, having accomplished this **feat** on five occasions. He briefly held the single-season record of 5,476 yards, set in 2011, until he was overtaken by Peyton Manning's 2013 season 5,477-yard performance.

Brees completes a 20-yard, 3rd-quarter pass to WR Willie Snead in a January 1, 2017, game against the Atlanta Falcons. The pass put Brees over the 5,000-yard mark for the season for the fifth time in his NFL career.

Brees has made 249 starts in seventeen NFL seasons.

RESEARCH PROJECT:

Drew Brees began his career as a member of the San Diego Chargers, which he played for during the 2001–2005 seasons, before accepting an offer to become the starter in New Orleans. Brees took over the starting role from a former Heisman Award winner, Doug Flutie, and was replaced by another QB star, Philip Rivers. For their careers, Brees and Rivers have combined for 120,793 yards passing and 830 touchdowns. Name two other pairs of quarterbacks who played immediately after each other who passed for at least 90,000 yards combined and over 600 touchdowns (hint: both pairs played for Midwestern teams).

TEXT-DEPENDENT QUESTIONS:

1. What school did Drew Brees play college football? What conference is the school a member?
2. What NFL record did Brees hold briefly before it was taken by QB Peyton Manning in 2013?
3. How many NFL career passing yards does Brees have? What is his ranking all-time for passing yards in the NFL?

WORDS TO UNDERSTAND

CONTEMPORARY – a person who lives at the same time or is about the same age as another person

CULMINATE – reaching the highest or a climactic or decisive point

INDUCTEES – people who have been officially made a member of a group or organization

NAMESAKE – one who is named after another or for whom another is named

PREP SPORTS – sports played at a usually private school preparing students primarily for college

CHAPTER 2

THE ROAD TO THE TOP

ATHLETIC ACCOMPLISHMENTS IN
HIGH SCHOOL AND COLLEGE

Andrew Christopher Brees was born in Austin, TX, on January 15, 1979. Dallas Cowboys WR Drew Pearson was a favorite of the family and, as a *Sports Illustrated* article claimed, was the **namesake** for young Brees. His parents, both attorneys, are Eugene Wilson "Chip" Brees II and Mina Brees, who died in 2009. Brees' parents divorced when he was seven, leaving him to spend time between two homes for much of his youth.

Drew Brees has two siblings: younger brother Reid and younger half-sister Audrey (Brees) Martin (born in 1989).

HIGH SCHOOL

Drew Brees played baseball, basketball, and football as a high school athlete, attending Westlake High School in Austin, TX. He attended the same high school that Philadelphia

In his senior year at Westlake High School in Austin, TX, Brees led the football team to a state title.

Eagles backup and Super Bowl LII winner Nick Foles attended. An ACL injury in Brees' junior year limited him as he considered a possible career in college baseball instead of football.

Brees came back to play QB in his senior year at Westlake for the Chaparrals. He completed his high school career as the Texas 5A High School Most Valuable Player. His Westlake team went a perfect 16–0 in 1996 and went on to become state champions. Brees received honorable mention to the state's High School All-Star team and to the *USA Today* All-USA high school team that also featured his future San Diego Chargers teammate, RB LaDainian Tomlinson.

Drew Brees posted these numbers during his years at Westlake, singling out his senior season in which he started every game:

Year(s)	Record	Comp	Attempts	Comp%	Yards	TDs
1993–1995	12–0–1	103	157	65.6	1,433	19
1996*	16–0–0	211	333	63.4	3,528	31
TOTAL	28–0–1	314	490	64.1	5,461	50

*Won Texas 5A State Championship.

Brees recovered from his knee injury to finish his high school career strong, with hopes of attending either Texas A&M University or the University of Texas in Austin to continue playing in the footsteps of his uncle and grandfather. He unfortunately received little interest from either program and received recruiting offers from Purdue University ("Boilermakers") and the University of Kentucky.

COLLEGE

Brees chose to attend Purdue based on their academic programs and a chance to play against Big Ten powerhouses like the University of Michigan, Ohio State University, Penn State University, and the University of Wisconsin. Brees saw limited action as a freshman, and it wasn't until his sophomore year that he became the regular starter for the Boilermakers.

Brees put up impressive numbers in the three years he started at QB for Purdue. He played in what has become an ESPN Classic matchup in 2000 against 12th-ranked Ohio State in his senior year on October 28, 2000. The Boilermakers, entering the game ranked 16th and a game back in the standings, more than held their own, winning by a final score of 31–27. Brees completed 39 passes against 65 attempts for 455 yards. He tossed 3 touchdowns and 4 interceptions.

SPORTS IS ALL IN THE BREES FAMILY

Brees is certainly the most famous athlete in his family, having been named a Super Bowl MVP and two-time AP Offensive Player of the Year. The family tree also includes several other athletes and members who are involved in sports. His brother Reid played baseball for four years at Baylor University where he was an All-Big 12 outfielder. His father Chip played basketball at Texas A&M University.

Drew Brees is not the only quarterback to have made it at the collegiate level; his uncle Marty Akins was a standout QB at the University of Texas from 1972–1975. He became captain of the Longhorn squad in 1975 and played (or participated) in four bowl games (Cotton Bowl twice, Bluebonnet Bowl, Gator Bowl). Akins ran the wishbone offense as a three-year starter for the Longhorns, playing in his senior year on the same team as Hall of Fame running back Earl Campbell. Atkins was drafted by the St. Louis Cardinals in 1976 and later traded to New Orleans, leaving professional football in 1977.

Brees' grandfather (Ray Akins) was a legendary high school coach and one of winningest head coaches in Texas history. He spent twenty-eight years as a coach and athletic director for the Gregory-Portland High School "Wildcats" in Portland, TX. A World War II Marine veteran who fought in Okinawa, Atkins accumulated 293 wins, making him one of the most successful coaches in Texas prep sports history.

Drew Brees' younger sister Audrey is very much involved in the world of sports as well, working with the broadcast team for the NBA on TNT as a social media manager.

A 2017 profile of Drew Brees' sister Audrey Brees, an Assistant Manager on the Social Media team for Turner Sports in Atlanta. Brees is responsible for maintaining the social media presence for the personalities of TNT's NBA on TNT show, via Snapchat, Twitter, Facebook, and other platforms.

Brees played college football for Purdue University at Ross-Ade Stadium in West Lafayette, IN.

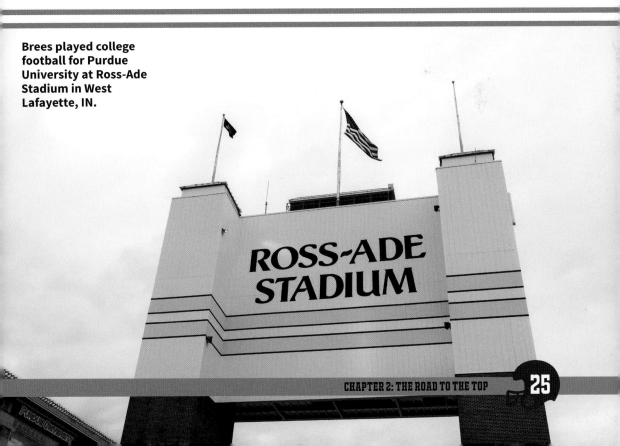

The victory, along with victories over the University of Michigan and Northwestern University, gave Purdue a share of the Big Ten championship and an invitation to play in the Rose Bowl against the 4th-ranked University of Washington. The game resulted in a 34–24 loss with Brees passing for 275 yards (23–39) with 2 touchdowns.

In his college career at Purdue, Brees set two NCAA passing records and 13 Big Ten Conference passing records as well as several school records for the university. His NCAA records include a tie for the longest touchdown pass (99 yards) and passing attempts in a single game (83), which stood until broken by QB Connor Halliday of Washington State University, who made 89 attempts against the University of Oregon on October 19, 2013.

Brees finished third in the voting for the 2000 Heisman Trophy, awarded to the best player in college football. That is one position ahead of future teammate LaDainian Tomlinson, whom the Chargers drafted one round ahead of Brees.

Here are the career stats for Brees for his four years at Purdue:

Season	Completions	Attempts	Comp%	Yards	TDs	INTs
1997	19	43	44.2	232	0	1
1998	361	569	63.4	3.983	39	20
1999	337	554	60.8	3,909	25	12
2000	309	512	60.4	3,668	26	12
TOTALS	1,026	1,678	61.1	11,792	90	45

Brees was named an Academic All-American in 2000 and was a three-time Academic All-Big Ten honoree. He was awarded the Maxwell Award in 2000, given to the most outstanding player in college football and finished third in the Heisman Award voting, just ahead of Tomlinson, who played at Texas Christian University.

NFL DRAFT DAY 2001

Brees entered the 2001 NFL Draft after his record setting college career, which **culminated** with an appearance in the 2001 Rose Bowl in Pasadena, CA, against the University of Washington Huskies. He participated in the 2001 NFL Scouting Combine, where he posted the following results:

- Measurements (height, weight): 6 feet 0 inches (1.83 m), 213 lb (96.6 kg)
- 40-yard dash: 4.85 seconds
- 3-cone: 7.09 seconds
- Vertical jump: 32.0 inches (0.81 m)
- Broad jump: 8 feet 9 inches (2.67 m)

Brees scored a 28 out of 50 on the famous Wonderlic test, just above the average score of 26 for quarterbacks.

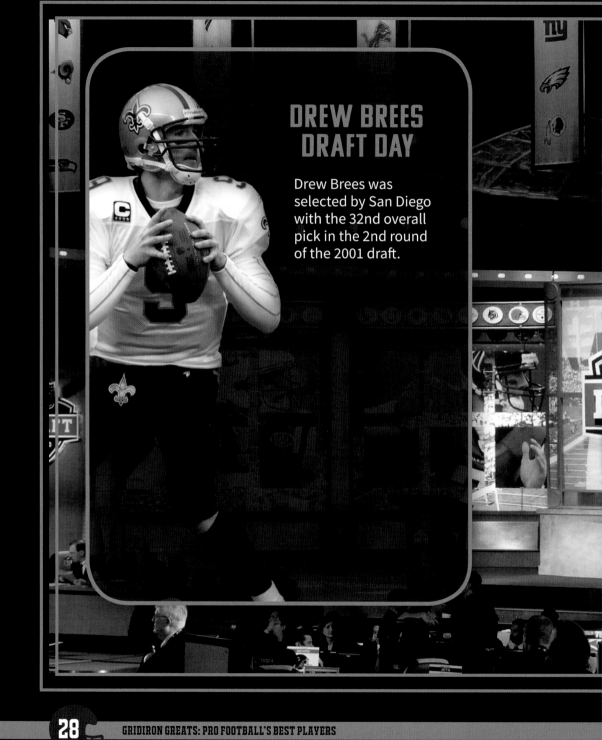

DREW BREES DRAFT DAY

Drew Brees was selected by San Diego with the 32nd overall pick in the 2nd round of the 2001 draft.

NFL DRAFT DAY 2001
SIGNIFICANT ACCOUNTS

The 2001 NFL Draft was held at the Theater at Madison Square Garden in New York City between April 21–22, 2001.

- A total of 246 players were chosen in seven rounds.

- QB Michael Vick of Virginia Tech University was the 1st overall draft selection, made by Atlanta Falcons.

- Brees was one of only eleven QBs taken in the 2001 NFL Draft.

- The Carolina Panthers drafted Chris Weinke of Florida State University, the Heisman Trophy winner from 2000, in the 4th round with the 106th selection. Weinke holds the second-longest career losing streak for NFL QBs and in seven seasons (with Carolina and the San Francisco 49ers), won 2 games total.

- Of the eleven quarterbacks selected in the 2001 NFL Draft, only Brees is still active in the NFL (2017).

- The Buffalo Bills and Seattle Seahawks each had twelve selections in the 2001 draft, the most of all NFL teams.

- Washington had the least amount of selections in the draft with five.

- The 2001 NFL Draft produced one member of Pro Football's Hall of Fame: RB LaDainian Tomlinson from TCU, selected 5th overall by the San Diego Chargers, twenty-seven picks ahead of Drew Brees. Tomlinson was inducted in 2017.

Doug Flutie was the starting QB in San Diego when Brees arrived in 2001.

RESEARCH PROJECT

Drew Brees comes from an athletic family, with both his parents having played high school and college sports and a brother who was a standout baseball player at the Baylor University. Additionally, Brees has an uncle, Marty Akins, who was also a star quarterback in college and was named an All-American in his senior year, while Brees earned Academic All-American honors in 2001 (and was inducted in the Academic All-American Hall of Fame in 2016). Name three current or former NFL players along with their relative who both were named to an All-American team in college (hint: find a list of NFL family relations to assist you in your research).

DREW BREES VS. OTHER TOP QUARTERBACKS

Drew Brees took over as San Diego's starter for an injured Doug Flutie in a game against Kansas City on November 4, 2001. He completed 15 of 27 passes thrown for 221 yards and his first career NFL touchdown, in a 25–20 loss. He eventually became the full-time starter for the San Diego Chargers, starting all sixteen games in 2002, posting an 8–8 win-loss record for the season.

From San Diego to New Orleans, Brees established him as one of the greatest passing quarterbacks the NFL has ever seen. Here are the stats of several **contemporaries** of Brees, including Tom Brady, Eli Manning, Ben Roethlisberger, and Aaron Rodgers, and how their careers compare:

NAME	TEAM(S)	YEARS	YARDS	COMP	ATTEMPTS	COMP%	TDS
Drew Brees (1)	San Diego, New Orleans	2001–2017	70,445	6,222	9,294	66.9	488
Tom Brady (5)	New England	2000–2017	66,159	5,629	8,805	63.9	488
Eli Manning (2)	NY Giants	2005–2017	51,682	4,424	7,396	59.8	339
Ben Roethlisberger (2)	Pittsburgh	2004–2017	51,065	4,164	6,493	64.1	329
Aaron Rodgers (1)	Green Bay	2008–2017	38,502	3,188	4,895	65.1	313

() – number of Super Bowl championships.

Drew Brees' career numbers are not only impressive when compared to some of the greatest Super Bowl winning quarterbacks playing in the NFL today but also against some of the all-time greatest quarterbacks. This includes several Hall of

Brees defeated all-time passing yards leader Peyton Manning in Super Bowl XLIV. Brees will likely break Manning's yardage record in 2018.

Fame **inductees** such as John Elway, Brett Favre, Eli's brother Peyton Manning (whom Brees faced in Super Bowl XLIV) and Dan Marino:

NAME	TEAM(S)	YEAR	YARDS	COMP	ATTEMPTS	COMP%	TDS
Peyton Manning (2)	Indianapolis, Denver	1998–2015	71,940	6,125	9,380	65.3	539
Brett Favre + (1)	Green Bay, NY Jets, Minnesota	1991–2010	71,838	6,300	10,169	62.0	508
Drew Brees (1)	San Diego, New Orleans	2001–2017	70,445	6,222	9,294	66.9	488
Dan Marino + (0)	Miami	1983–1999	61,361	4,967	8,358	59.4	420
John Elway + (2)	Denver	1983–1998	51475	4,123	7,250	56.9	300

+ - Hall of Fame inductees.

DREW BREES VS. PHILIP RIVERS

Brees left the Chargers after the 2005 season and became the starting quarterback in New Orleans. His replacement in San Diego was Philip Rivers, the 4th pick and second quarterback taken (behind Eli Manning of the NY Giants) at the 2004 NFL Draft. Rivers sat behind Brees during his comeback year of 2004 and took the starting job in 2006 after Brees left for the Saints. Rivers led the team to a 14-win 2006 and an 11-win 2007 season, winning the AFC West both years but suffering AFC Championship losses to New England twice.

Here is a look at what Rivers has accomplished in his fourteen-year career with the Chargers in comparison to Brees NFL career:

Philip Rivers took over as QB in San Diego after Brees left for New Orleans.

NAME	TEAM(S)	YEAR	YARDS	COMP	ATTEMPTS	COMP%	TDS
Drew Brees	San Diego, New Orleans	2001–2017	70,445	6,222	9,294	66.9	488
Philip Rivers	San Diego/ LA Chargers	2004–2017	50,348	4,171	6,492	64.2	342

Here's an additional comparison of the accomplishments of Brees and Rivers over their respective NFL careers:

- Super Bowl wins: Brees (1), Rivers (0)
- Super Bowl MVPs: Brees (1), Rivers (0)
- NFL Offensive Player of the Year: Brees (2), Rivers (0)
- NFL Comeback Player of the Year: Brees (1, 2004), Rivers (1, 2013)
- Pro Bowl Appearances: Brees (11), Rivers (7)
- All-Pro Selections: Brees (4, 1 First-Team, 3 Second-Team), Rivers (2, 1 First-Team, 1 Second-Team)

TEXT-DEPENDENT QUESTIONS:

1. How many quarterbacks were selected in the 2001 NFL Draft? How many QBs drafted in 2001 were still in the NFL as of the end of the 2017 season?

2. How many school and BigTen records did Drew Brees set while attending Purdue University?

3. How many touchdown passes has Drew Brees thrown in his NFL career (as of the end of 2017)? What quarterback is he tied with for career touchdowns?

WORDS TO UNDERSTAND

ACCOUNT – to be the sole or primary factor

AMASSED – gathered or collected

PAR – at the same level

PROLIFIC – very inventive or productive

CHAPTER 3

ON THE FIELD

DREW BREES' NFL ACCOMPLISHMENTS

Drew Brees has had seventeen very successful seasons in the NFL. His numbers are on **par** with some of the greatest QBs who have played in the NFL. He is one of the most **prolific** passers in the history of the game and is one of the game's statistical leaders in several categories such as touchdowns, pass completions, pass attempts, and yards.

DREW BREES' CAREER PASSING STATISTICS

Drew Brees is the only quarterback in NFL history to pass for 5,000 yards or more in a single season multiple times. In fact, Brees has accomplished this milestone in five different seasons (2008, 2011–2013, 2016). Those 26,092 yards from the five NFL seasons he passed for 5,000 or more yards **account** for more than a third (37%) of his career passing yard total of 70,445.

His 5,476 yards passing in 2011 were the most in NFL history for a single season until Peyton Manning passed for 5,477 in 2013. Brees is one of only five quarterbacks to reach the 5,000-yard passing mark. Hall of Fame and Miami Dolphins great Dan Marino was the first to accomplish this feat in 1984. The members of the 5,000-yard passing club include:

Player	Team	Yards	Year
Peyton Manning	Denver Broncos	5,477	2013
Drew Brees	New Orleans Saints	5,476	2011
Tom Brady	New England Patriots	5,235	2011
Drew Brees	New Orleans Saints	5,208	2016
Drew Brees	New Orleans Saints	5,177	2012
Drew Brees	New Orleans Saints	5,162	2013
Dan Marino	Miami Dolphins	5,084	1984
Drew Brees	New Orleans Saints	5,069	2008
Matthew Stafford	Detroit Lions	5,038	2011

Drew Brees is one of only three quarterbacks in NFL history who has passed for 70,000 or more yards in his career. His total of 70,445 puts him behind former Green Bay Packer and Indianapolis Colts/Denver Broncos greats Brett Favre and Peyton Manning as the only QBs with that accomplishment. Brees is within 1,495 yards of Peyton Manning's all-time record of 71,440. Given his seventeen-year average of over 4,000 yards passing per season, it should take Brees no more than six games in the 2018 NFL season to set a new NFL career passing-yard record.

Brees led the league in total offense (passing, rushing, receiving) in five of his seventeen NFL seasons (2008, 2011, 2012, 2015, and 2016). He is the active total offense leader and ranks third all-time in total offensive production with 68,489 yards. Brees

Brees has passed for more than 5,000 yards in a season a record five times. No other player has done so more than once.

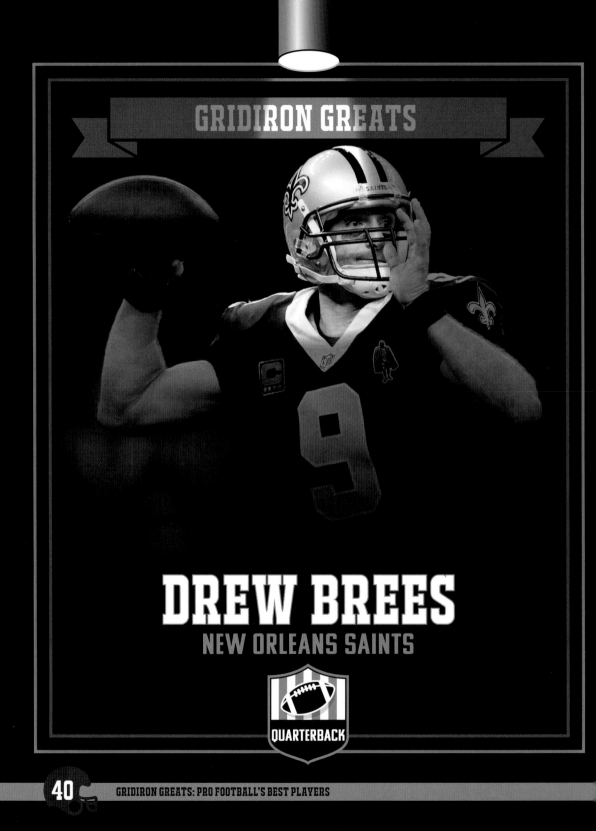

GRIDIRON GREATS

DREW BREES
NEW ORLEANS SAINTS

QUARTERBACK

DREW BREES

Date of birth: January 15, 1979
Height: 6 feet, 0 inches (1.83 m), **Weight:** Approx. 209 lb (95 kg)
Drafted in the 2nd round in 2001 (32nd pick overall) by the San Diego Chargers
College: Purdue University

CAREER

Games	Completions	Attempts	Comp%	Yards	TDs	INT
249	6,222	9.,294	66.9	70,445	488	228

- Named to 11 Pro Bowls (2004, 2006, 2008–2014, 2016–2017)
- Named First-Team All-Pro once (2006)
- Named Second-Team All-Pro three times (2008, 2009, 2011)
- Named NFL Bert Bell Award Player of the Year in 2009
- Named NFL Associated Press Offensive Player of the Year twice (2008, 2011)
- Named NFL AP Comeback Player of the Year (2004)
- Named NFL Walter Payton Man of the Year (2006)
- Named Super Bowl MVP (XLIV), 2010
- Named Big Ten Offensive Player of the Year twice (1998, 2000)
- Winner of the Maxwell Award for Most Outstanding College Player (2000)

QUARTERBACK

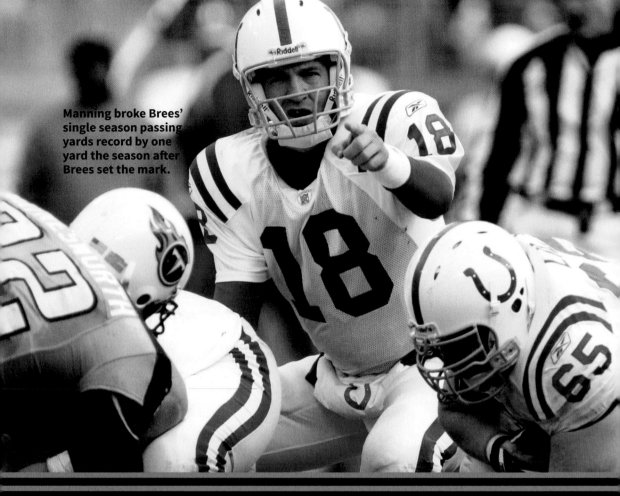

Manning broke Brees' single season passing yards record by one yard the season after Brees set the mark.

RESEARCH PROJECT

Drew Brees earned the Maxwell Award as the Player of the Year in college football as a senior at Purdue University in 2000. Eleven years later (2009), as a member of the New Orleans Saints, Brees was recognizes with the Bert Bell Award as the Player of the Year for the NFL. Name three other players who won the Maxwell Award in college and the Bert Bell Award in the NFL (Hint: one of the three has won the Bert Bell Award multiple times).

also led the league pass-completion percentage four times in his NFL career (2009, 2010, 2011, and 2017). He is both the active and career pass-completion-percentage leader at 66.9%. He has played in 249 career games and has started 248, ranked 13th all-time. Drew Brees is near or at the top of the career statistical categories for NFL quarterbacks.

A look at his career number in pass completions, attempts, yards, touchdowns, and completion percentage rank him one, two, or three all-time. Brees has an opportunity to become the top passer in league's history in all categories before his NFL career comes to a close.

No active player has more pass attempts than Brees' 9,294 (through 2017).

- Pass Completions – Ranked second with 6,222 completions; Brett Favre (1), 6,300.
- Pass Attempts – Ranked second with 9,294 passing attempts; Brett Favre (1), 10,169.
- Passing Yards – Ranked third with 70,445 yards; Peyton Manning (1), 71,940.
- Touchdowns – Tied for third (with Tom Brady) with 488 touchdowns; Peyton Manning (1), 539.
- Completion Percentage – Ranked first with 66.9% completion percentage; Chad Pennington (2), 66%.

THE IMPORTANCE OF SUPER BOWL XLIV WIN FOR CITY OF NEW ORLEANS

New Orleans has always had a reputation, beyond the beads and parades of Mardi Gras, as being a tough place to live. It became even more difficult a place when the effects of Hurricane Katrina in August–September 2005 devastated the city, causing widespread damage and destruction. Nearly two thousand residents lost their lives in the storm, and it took many years for the city to recover from the financial and emotional cost of the storm.

The 2009 season was a special one for the Saints. Four years after Katrina, the team, led by Brees and his 4,388 passing yards and 34 touchdowns, won its first thirteen games on its way to a 13–3 regular season and number one seed in the NFC playoffs. Victories over a Brett Favre-led Minnesota Vikings in the divisional round and Kurt Warner and the Arizona Cardinals in the NFC Championship game set up a Super Bowl matchup against Peyton Manning and the Indianapolis Colts.

Brees held form, completing 82 percent of his passes and tossing 2 touchdowns as the Saints defeated the Colts 31–17 for the team's (and city's) first championship. President Barack Obama summed up his feelings about the game and its special meaning by saying, "I do have a soft spot in my heart for New Orleans, mainly because of what the city's gone through over these last several years, and I just know how much that team means to them."

Drew Brees is seen with his son Baylen at the end of his effort leading the New Orleans Saints to a 31–17 win in Super Bowl XLIV. The moment was a special one for Brees, the game's MVP, who was quoted in saying, "We played for so much more than ourselves."

DREW BREES HONORS, ACCOMPLISHMENTS, AND AWARDS

Drew Brees has **amassed** various records and honors over the course of seventeen seasons in the NFL playing for both San Diego and New Orleans. He has been named the MVP of a Super Bowl, received the Bert Bell Award (more on that below), and been a member of eleven Pro Bowl teams. He was also named a first-team All-Pro in 2006.

Here is a list of honors, accomplishments, and awards that Drew Brees has accumulated as a QB in the NFL:

- NFL's active leader in passing attempts with 9,294, through the 2017 NFL season.
- NFL's active leader in pass completions with 6,222 through the 2017 NFL season.
- NFL's co-active leader in touchdowns with 488 through the 2017 NFL season.

- Led the NFL four times in touchdown passes thrown, 2008, 2009, 2011, and 2012.
- Named the NFL's Comeback Player of the Year in 2004 while with San Diego.
- Won the NFL's Walter Payton Man of the Year Award, given to players for their service to the community, in 2006, along with former teammate LaDainian Tomlinson.
- Won the NFL's AP Offensive Player of the Year Award twice in his career, 2008 and 2011.

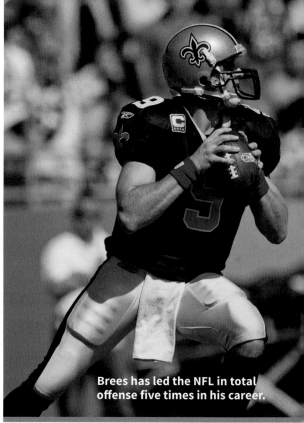

Brees has led the NFL in total offense five times in his career.

Drew Brees was also named AFC Offensive Player of the Week twice and the NFC's Offensive Player of the Week twenty times.

BERT BELL AWARD

Brees was named the Bert Bell Award winner for the 2009 season, in which he led the New Orleans Saints to their first Super Bowl championship. The Bert Bell Award is named after former NFL Commissioner Bert Bell. It is given to the league's Player of the Year. The award is presented by the Maxwell Club, which was founded by Bert Bell and also gives the Maxwell Award to the Player of the Year in college. Brees was also recognized with the Maxwell Award as QB for the Purdue University Boilermakers in 2000.

Brees was the winner of the 2009 Bert Bell Award as NFL Player of the Year, an award named for the former NFL commissioner, seen here on the right signing the paperwork for purchase of the Dallas Texans franchise in 1952.

TEXT-DEPENDENT QUESTIONS:

1. 1. What year was Drew Brees named a first-team All-Pro? How many Pro Bowl teams was Drew Brees named?

2. 2. How many times did Brees earn Player of the Week offensive honors in the NFC? How many total times did Brees win Offensive Player of the Week honors?

3. 3. How many seasons did Brees pass for at least 5,000 yards? How many quarterbacks (in addition to Brees) in NFL history passed for 5,000 yards in a single season?

WORDS TO UNDERSTAND

EVIDENT – something that is obvious and clear

INTERTWINED – very closely involved with each other

LABRUM – a piece of fibrous cartilage that holds the ball joint of the shoulder in the shoulder socket

NEGOTIATE – to create a solution or agreement by way of discussion

STATURE – natural height (as of a person) in an upright position

CHAPTER 4

WORDS COUNT

When the time comes to address the media before or after a game, players either retreat to the comfort of traditional phrases that avoid controversy (Cliché City), or they speak their mind with refreshing candor (Quote Machine).

Here are ten quotes from Drew Brees, compiled in part from the website 247Sports.com (and other websites), with some insight as to the context of what he is talking about or referencing:

Brees has put up numbers in his NFL career that rank him among the best active or retired quarterbacks in the history of the game. His totals for passing completions, pass attempts, passing yards, touchdowns, and other categories place him among the top QBs and all but assures his entry into the Hall of Fame when he leaves the game. As easy as it would be for him to simply rest on his past accomplishments, Brees knows that he can always do a little more and become a little better to achieve success. He could be a little bit better in expressing this. **Rating: Cliché City**

> "You can always be a little bit better."

"And at the time, it is funny how you can look at something and say, for example with my shoulder injury, when it first happened I said this is the worst thing that could happen to me. Why me, why now? Now I look back and say it was probably the best thing that happssaened to me"

Rivers in 2006, the year he took over in San Diego after Brees left. Rivers has a total of four playoff wins in twelve seasons as the Charger' starter.

Brees injured his **labrum**, the cartilage that keeps the ball of the shoulder bone in the socket, in a December 31, 2005, game against the Denver Broncos. The injury required four months to heal and placed doubt on Brees' ability to continue in the role of the Chargers' starting QB. Philip Rivers, the team's high draft pick from 2004, stepped into the role and when it came time to **negotiate** Brees' contract; he felt he could get a better offer from other teams. The Chargers used the opportunity to permanently install Rivers as the new starting QB, and as for Brees, he accepted an offer to play in New Orleans, which resulted in multiple Offensive Player of the Year awards, nine additional Pro Bowl selections, and a Super Bowl Championship.
Rating: Quote Machine

"We all understand what we signed up for, but then again, you don't want this to be a game that puts people in wheelchairs at age forty."

As many players in the NFL understand, Brees knows that football is a violent sport. Injury is a part of the game and it's one of the costs players pay to play at this level. Issues such as concussions and recurring injuries that have crippled some players in retirement are a concern many players have and have organizations like the NFL Players Association and other groups advocating for more rules that ensure safety on the field and the appropriate type of equipment to lower the possibility of ending up in a wheelchair at the end of a playing career. **Rating: Quote Machine**

"I obviously take a lot of pride in what I do on the football field, because that has the ability to influence a lot of people. That puts smiles on people's faces. That gives people a pep in their step on Monday morning when they go back to work."

Winning games on Sunday is the way Brees contributes to helping the fans of New Orleans feel better about their lives during football season. There is no doubt about the way the members of the Who Dat Nation, as Saints fans are known, feel about their quarterback. During the Super Bowl XLIV-winning season of 2009, songs and anthems were written about Brees and the Saints as a tribute and appreciation for the effort the team was putting forth to bring the city together. **Rating: Quote Machine**

"It has been an interesting road, but I wouldn't trade any of it for the world, because I feel like all of those instances in my life I felt molded me and strengthened me and made me who I am."

Brees again expresses a key sentiment in an unoriginal way, but he has had to overcome disappointment and adversity throughout his life and career. He wasn't a highly sought-after recruit coming out of high school. He was taken in the second round of the 2001 NFL Draft and played behind an established quarterback in Heisman Trophy winner Doug Flutie, until injury thrust Brees into the starting role in 2002. A shoulder injury Brees suffered at the end of the 2005 season brought about a move from the team that drafted him to the Crescent City, a nickname for New Orleans. The city where he would spend the next twelve years of his career had just suffered the devastation of Hurricane Katrina in the fall of 2005 and would take years to recover. All of his experiences, he feels, have shaped him into the player he has become. **Rating: Cliché City**

Brees persevered through adversity in his career before achieving superstar status with the Saints.

Drew Brees and LaDainian Tomlinson were great players in the State of Texas, respective 4A and 5A Most Outstanding Players in 1996. Had any of the Texas colleges and universities shown interest in Drew Brees coming out of Austin's Westlake High School, it may have been possible that the two would have been college as well as NFL teammates. Here is an interesting research project: find five pairs of players who played together in college who went on to both be drafted in the first round of the same NFL Draft.

"Sometimes all you need is just somebody to believe in you in order to be able to accomplish maybe what you never thought you could."

This quote is at the heart of who Brees is as a successful NFL quarterback and as a person. Brees led his Austin, TX, high school team to a perfect 16–0 record and a Texas 5A state championship, as well as being named the Texas 5A Most Outstanding Player. These credentials should have been more than enough to get him noticed by in-state schools like the University of Texas and Texas A&M University. He instead only received interest from the University of Kentucky and Purdue University, where he chose to attend and ended up winning a Big Ten championship in his senior year (2000) and the Maxwell Award for college football's Player of the Year. Although he explains it in an unoriginal way, Purdue's belief in his ability to play QB was the opening Brees needed to accomplish his dreams and become one of the best athletes to play in the NFL. **Rating: Cliché City**

> **"There's always a little bit of personal satisfaction when you prove somebody wrong."**

Brees has made a career out of disproving people's expectations about him and his abilities, both as a quarterback and as a leader. He stands at just 6 feet tall (1.83 m) and 209 lb (95 kg), making him small in **stature** in comparison with other NFL quarterbacks. Brees is one of only three active NFL QBs who is shorter than 6' 2" (1.88 m). The other two are Tyrod Taylor of the Buffalo Bills at 6'1"(1.85 m) and Russell Wilson of the Seattle Seahawks at 5'11" (1.8 m). Despite his size and questions about his arm strength and other qualities, Brees has lasted seventeen years in the NFL, amassing many honors and records along the way. **Rating: Quote Machine**

Seattle's Russell Wilson is one of the rare starting QBs in the NFL shorter than Brees.

"A good friend of mine once told me that each morning when you wake up, think about winning the day. Don't worry about a week from now or a month from now—just think about one day at a time. If you are worried about the mountain in the distance, you might trip over the molehill right in front of you. Win the day!"

This quote from Brees is a reminder to himself to always stay in the moment and focus on what is right in front of you. Keeping his focus on the immediate task at hand helps remove the worry about what's to come, which may be too far off in the distance to effect. By doing the little immediate things, you can stay in control and earn the larger victories in the future. The quote is motivational, but not very original. **Rating: Cliché City**

"I was brought here [New Orleans] for a reason. I feel like I can make a tremendous impact, not only with the team but in the community."

Brees appreciates the twelve seasons he has spent as the QB of the New Orleans Saints. His career has taken off since joining the Saints in 2006, and the free-agency move has led to records, recognition, and a Super Bowl championship. This quote is acknowledgement of not only how coming to New Orleans has allowed him to have an impact on the field, but also how it has allowed him to leave his mark in the Greater New Orleans community. **Rating: Quote Machine**

A home in New Orleans sits destroyed following hurricane Katrina in 2005. Brees came to the city the following year and became heavily involved with recovery efforts in the community.

The devastation of Hurricane Katrina in 2005 took many years to be fixed. It also took a while to bring back the life and morale of the city known for its annual Mardi Gras festival, music, food, and good times (as they say in New Orleans, "laissez les bon temps rouler"—let the good times roll!). Winning Super Bowl XLIV was the spark that New Orleans needed to revive the spirit of Crescent City. Brees' remark captures the feeling of a moment like winning the championship for something larger than just the team. **Rating: Quote Machine**

"**We just believed in ourselves, and we knew that we had an entire city and maybe an entire country behind us. What can I say? I tried to imagine what this moment would be like for a long time, and it's better than expected.**"

LADAINIAN TOMLINSON ON DREW BREES' NFL SUCCESS

LaDainian Tomlinson is a huge fan of Drew Brees. The two players spent five seasons together playing for the San Diego Chargers, 2001–2005, and worked out together in the offseason with the same trainer. Of those sessions, Tomlinson commented that, "Our (offseason) trainer used to, with Drew and I, every drill we would challenge each other, or he would make us compete against each other. If Drew lost against me, he wanted to do it again. It was like one of those things (he would say), 'Oh, let's do it one more time.' I'm like, 'No, Drew. I'm done. I'm tired.' But he never seemed to get tired. That's just his competitive nature. He did not want to lose."

Tomlinson, who retired after eleven seasons, sees the competitive spirit and winning demeanor that Brees brings to the game. He is not surprised by his success and ability to continue playing, even after seventeen NFL seasons. Tomlinson did remark, in a February 2, 2017, interview with New Orleans's *The Times-Picayune* that " . . . it's killing him not to be at least competing for a division title, competing to get in the playoffs and win an NFC Championship and get back to another Super Bowl."

DREW BREES AND LADAINIAN TOMLINSON

Perhaps no two playing careers in the NFL were so **intertwined** as those of Brees and LaDainian Tomlinson. Tomlinson, a fellow Texas prep star, played for University High School in Waco, TX, at the same time Brees was leading Westlake High School in Austin.

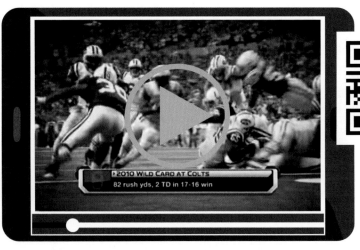

Drew Brees on the receiving end of LaDainian Tomlinson's first NFL pass in a game against the Oakland Raiders, on September 28, 2003. [Begin at the 0:017 second mark]

Tomlinson was named Texas 4A Most Outstanding Player in the same year Brees received 5A honors and both players were named Texas all-stars.

Tomlinson, a highly sought-after recruit, went to play at Texas Christian University in Fort Worth, TX, as Brees went off to Purdue, where he became a consensus All-American. Tomlinson also received the Doak Walker award for the nation's best collegiate running back in 2000. He left college with the third-most rushing yards in a game against the University of Texas at El Paso (406) in 1999, a record he held until future Los Angeles Chargers running back Melvin Gordon from the University of Wisconsin outrushed him in 2014 for 408 yards and University of Oklahoma's Samaje Perine established a new mark of 427 yards the week after.

Tomlinson and Brees were both drafted by the San Diego Chargers in the 2001 NFL Draft; Tomlinson was selected with the 5th overall pick in the 1st round and Brees with the 32nd overall pick in the 2nd round. The tandem of Brees and Tomlinson went on to turn the Chargers into a perennial AFC powerhouse. The year after Drew Brees went to play in

New Orleans, Tomlinson won the Most Valuable Player Award in 2006, rushing for 2,323 yards and 31 total touchdowns (28 rushing, 3 receiving). His 186 points scored in 2006 shattered the record held by former Green Bay Packer TE Paul Hornung for nearly fifty years.

The bond between the two players was never more **evident** than the two being named co-Walter Payton Man of the Year recipients for their community work in 2006. Tomlinson played a total of eleven seasons in the NFL, retiring after the 2011 season at 6th all-time on the NFL career rushing yards list with 13,684. His accomplishments on the field and record setting 2006 season put him in football's Hall of Fame in August of 2017.

Hall of Fame RB LaDainian Tomlinson (#21) played five seasons with Brees in San Diego.

TEXT-DEPENDENT QUESTIONS:

1. What NFL award did Drew Brees share with former teammate LaDainian Tomlinson in 2006?

2. What nickname is given to fans of the New Orleans Saints? What is the nickname for New Orleans, LA?

3. What season did Drew Brees suffer an injury to his shoulder?

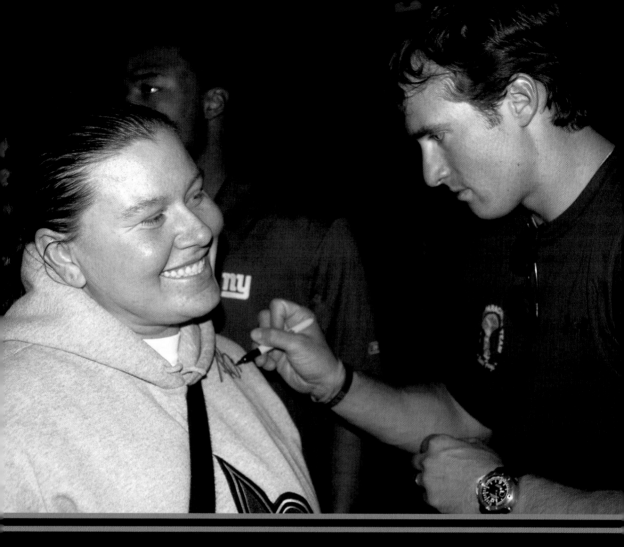

WORDS TO UNDERSTAND

INSEPARABLE – always together and/or bound together tightly

INTERACT – engaging in an exchange with another person, such as a conversation

REVIVE – bring back to life

WALK-ON – a college athlete who was not previously recruited or given a scholarship to participate on a team

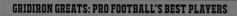

CHAPTER 5

OFF THE FIELD

THE BREES' HOME LIFE

Drew Brees moved into Uptown New Orleans not too long after accepting an offer to play for the Saints in 2006. The city was still in the process of recovering from hurricane related damages and **reviving** its sense of community, culture, and heritage. The Uptown neighborhood includes Tulane University, home to Yulman Stadium, which the Saints use for preseason practice. The stadium also happens to be close to Brees' home, allowing him to walk home from practice and **interact** with young Saints fans on the way.

Brees married his longtime girlfriend Brittany Dudchenko in 2003. The couple first met in 1998, when both were sophomores attending Purdue University. **Inseparable** ever since, they welcomed their first child, a son named Baylen Robert, on January 15, 2009. They have four children together, three sons and a daughter. In addition to Baylen is Bowen Christopher (born October 19, 2010), Callen Christopher (born August 15, 2012), and Rylen Judith (born August 25, 2014).

THE BREES FAMILY

Brees and his wife Brittany at the 2012 ESPY Awards show in Los Angeles.

After Brees' parents split when he was seven, Brees and his brother Reid split their time between two homes, that of his father Chip and mother Mina. A product of divorce, Brees had a difficult time growing up and having to go back and forth between his parents. A result of the divorce however was the close relationship Drew Brees developed with his brother Reid. His father, a prominent Austin-area trial attorney and partner with the firm Whitehurst, Harkness, Brees, Cheng, Alsaffar, Higginbotham, and Jacob, PLLC, would later remarry Amy Hightower and have a daughter, Brees' younger sister Audrey.

Brees' mother Mina was also an Austin attorney who ran for a seat on the Texas Third Court of Appeals as a judge in 2006. The relationship between Brees and his mother was strained, due to a desire, Brees claimed, of his mother's to represent him as his agent when he was drafted in 2000 by San Diego. She also used his image in campaign ads without his consent in 2006. The relationship between the two was rebuilding when his mother died unexpectedly on August 7, 2009, at the age of fifty-nine.

DREW BREES THE ENTREPRENEUR

In addition to his success on the football team, Brees has put much energy into building a career for himself as a business owner. Since coming to New Orleans with a contract that paid him $60 million over six years, including an $8 million signing bonus and $12 million option bonus for 2007, Brees has been active in the business community, investing in various restaurant franchises and a clothing store.

Brees owns two Jimmy John's franchise stores in New Orleans as part of his substantial business holdings.

WALK-ONS

Walk-ons Bistreaux & Bar, with fourteen locations across the State of Louisiana, and three Texas locations, opened to the public on September 9, 2003, near LSU's Tigers Stadium in Baton Rouge, LA. The restaurant's founders, Brandon Landry and Jack Warner, were teammates on the basketball team at LSU. As walk-ons the pair developed a close friendship that led to the creation of what would become a restaurant empire named Walk-ons.

The restaurant became a favorite of the newly arrived Drew Brees when he arrived in New Orleans in 2006. He was so impressed with the place that by 2015 he became a co-owner in the business, putting his money to work to help expand Walk-ons through the opening of additional locations in Louisiana and in Texas.

Video presentation about the story of Walk-ons Bistreaux & Bar founders Brandon Landry and Jack Warner, hosted by ESPN's Scott Van Pelt.

JIMMY JOHN'S GOURMET SANDWICH SHOPS

Jimmy John's Gourmet Sandwich Shops was a concept created by founder Jimmy John Liautaud in 1982. Graduating from high school with a loan from his father to open a business and turn a profit in the first year or join the US Army, he shopped for equipment to open a hot dog stand on the streets of Chicago's Downtown Loop. When he came across sandwich-making equipment instead that was within his budget, Jimmy John's sandwiches were born.

He located his first store near Eastern Illinois University in Charleston, IL, in January 1983. Since opening the Charleston store, Jimmy John's has grown to over 2,600 stores across the United States, worth more than $2 billion. Two stores located in the City of New Orleans on Elmwood and Maple Street and a location in Metairie, LA, (a suburb of New Orleans) on Veteran's Memorial Boulevard are owned by Drew Brees as part of his restaurant holdings.

Carl Buergler, first director of operations and now chief operating officer for Jimmy Johns, was Brees' backup at QB while the two attended Purdue University. Although

RESEARCH PROJECT

Drew Brees is one of the few players not only in the NFL but in pro sports who has been able to leverage his success on the field into success off it as a business owner and entrepreneur. Name three other professional athletes (NFL, NBA, MLB, PGA, etc.) who have been able to leverage their on the field/court earnings into successful businesses, providing detailed examples.

Buergler's football career never took off quite the same as Brees' did, the two reconnected years later when Drew Brees expressed an interest in opening a Jimmy John's in New Orleans. After signing his contract extension in July of 2012, Brees stopped by one of his New Orleans stores to take pictures with happy fans, sign autographs, and pick up sandwiches for the family.

DUNKIN' DONUTS

Brees is also a partner in several Dunkin' Donuts franchise stores.

Drew Brees became partners with FOX Sports announcer and former New York Giants lineman David Diehl and business owner Vik Patel to form Bourbon Street Donuts, LLC in 2016. The company owns forty-six Dunkin Donuts franchises throughout Alabama, Florida, and Louisiana.

Five stores were launched in Louisiana in 2017, and the partnership, along with Dunkin Donuts, announced plans for the opening of another sixty-four stores. The plan is to expand the Dunkin Donut brand throughout the southeastern United States in New Orleans, Baton Rouge, Shreveport, Monroe, and Alexandria, LA, over the next several years.

LIFESTYLE APPAREL COMPANY—9 BRAND STORES

Taking after his uniform number "9," Brees and wife Brittany launched a lifestyle apparel company in 2012 based in New Orleans called 9 Brand. The intention of the store is to provide an outlet for the charitable giving of the Brees family (see **Giving Back to the**

Community). A statement provided by the store states that, "9% of net proceeds from all 9 Brand products will be donated to the Brees Dream Foundation to support organizations focused on resilience. Proceeds from the first product line, the "ALL-IN" t-shirt, will be donated to organizations focused on Hurricane Isaac recovery in the Gulf Coast region."

HAPPY'S IRISH PUB

Brees entered into another partnership with Brandon Laundry of Walk-Ons, along with Rick Farrell, a New Orleans businessman, who took over Jack Warner's partnership interest in Walk-Ons in 2014. Farrell, who also owns the building that Walk-Ons is located in downtown New Orleans, is also a former **walk-on** himself for the LSU Tigers' baseball team in 1979. Happy's Irish Pub is located in Baton Rouge, having formerly had two locations in New Orleans, which have been closed.

GIVING BACK TO THE COMMUNITY

Drew Brees believes strongly in giving back to the community. Through his seventeen years playing football in the NFL, he has been given an opportunity to earn more money than most people will see in their lifetimes. Not only has he made nearly $170 million in salary and bonuses playing for both the San Diego Chargers and New Orleans Saints, he has used his money to build several businesses and stay invested in the community.

THE BREES DREAM FOUNDATION

The Brees Dream Foundation was created in 2003 as a way to extend Drew Brees personal mission for charitable giving on a global scale. The organization's stated mission is to partner with companies and other organizations in these areas of need:

- Cancer patients – to help improve the quality of life for patients suffering from cancer.
- Children and families in need – to fund efforts that provide care, education, and opportunities for families and children who are in need.

Since its beginning in 2003, the foundation has raised more than $25 million globally. Some of the organizations that have benefitted from financial assistance provided from the Brees Dream Foundation include:

- 9th Ward Field of Dreams – a New Orleans community-based organization founded in 2007 in the wake of the devastation to the Lower Ninth Ward neighborhood after Hurricane Katrina. The organization's purpose is to provide athletic facilities to Lower Ninth Ward youth.
- American Cancer Society – an Atlanta, GA-based organization founded in 1913, whose purpose is to eliminate cancer.
- Boys and Girls Club of Southeast Louisiana – an organization dedicated to providing programs and activities for youth to keep them engaged and off the streets.
- Convoy of Hope – a humanitarian and faith-based organization dedicated to providing food, water, supplies, and hope to impoverished communities.
- Kaboom! – a Washington, DC-based non-profit that works to increase activity for school-aged children by building playgrounds and installing playground equipment.

The American Cancer Society is a favorite cause that Brees supports through his Brees Dream Foundation.

- KIPP New Orleans Inc. – a college preparatory, independent charter school in New Orleans.
- Louisiana Fire Juniors – the official youth soccer club of the Chicago Fire of Major League Soccer.
- Ochsner Clinic Foundation – a non-profit multispecialty healthcare service in New Orleans.
- St. Michael Special School – a faith-based special education school located in New Orleans.
- Teach For America – a Washington, DC-based national organization dedicated to recruiting and developing a corps of teachers who teach in the nation's low-income schools.
- Tulane Athletics – the athletics program for Tulane University, located in Brees' Uptown neighborhood.
- Volunteers of America – a faith-based organization that provides affordable housing and housing assistance to low-income individuals living in the United States.

OTHER WORK AND RECOGNITION

Brees was the recipient of the Dungy-Thompson Humanitarian Award in 2012. The award is named in honor of former Big Ten player and former Tampa Bay Buccaneers and Super Bowl XLI winning coach (Indianapolis Colts) Tony Dungy (who played football for the University of Minnesota) and former NFL running back Anthony Thompson, who was a Walter Camp and Maxwell Award winner at Indiana University. It is given to a former Big Ten player in recognition of their charitable work.

Brees was also named the co-recipient of the Walter Payton Man of the Year Award in 2006 along with former teammate LaDainian Tomlinson. Brees was recognized for his efforts in his new community of New Orleans, which he arrived in the months after the devastating effects of Katrina. He partnered with a teammate, running back Deuce McAllister, to rebuild youth athletic facilities in New Orleans destroyed by the storm. Brees was also honored for continuing his charitable works in San Diego, sponsoring a golf tournament whose proceeds go to San Diego Children's Hospital and Cancer Research.

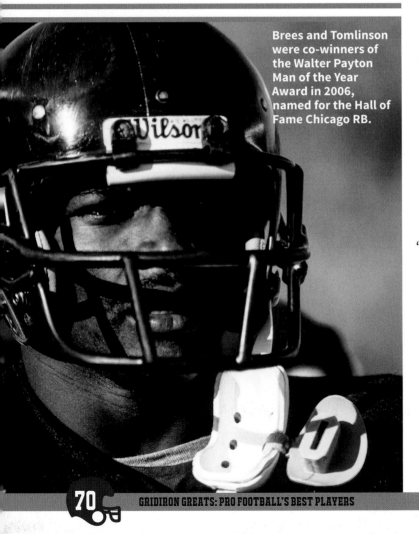

Brees and Tomlinson were co-winners of the Walter Payton Man of the Year Award in 2006, named for the Hall of Fame Chicago RB.

Brees has gone on five United Services Organization trips, visiting troops deployed in countries across the world, from Iraq and Afghanistan to Turkey and Guantanamo Bay. The USO is a nonprofit organization that works to boost troop morale by "keeping them connected to family, home and country, throughout their service to the nation." It is the kind of work that Brees has claimed to take more pride in helping with than any of his on-field successes.

Brees poses with a soldier during a USO tour stop in Kuwait in 2007.

TEXT-DEPENDENT QUESTIONS:

1. What is the name of the Drew Brees partnership with Vik Patel and former New York Giants lineman David Diehl? How many Dunkin Donuts partnerships does the partnership plan to open?

2. What are three organizations that have benefitted from the Brees Dream Foundation?

3. What is the name of the Brees charitable foundation? What is the mission of his charity?

SERIES GLOSSARY
OF KEY TERMS:

blitz – a defensive strategy in which one or more linebackers or defensive backs, in addition to the defensive line, attempt to overwhelm the quarterback's protection by attacking from unexpected locations or situations.

cornerbacks – the defenders primarily responsible for preventing the offenses wide receivers from catching passes, accomplished by remaining as close to the opponent as possible during pass routes. Cornerbacks are usually the fastest players on the defense.

defensive backs – a label applied to cornerbacks and safeties, or the secondary in general.

end zone – an area 10 yards deep at either end of the field bordered by the goal line and the boundaries.

field goal – an attempt to kick the ball through the uprights, worth three points. It is taken by a specialist called the place kicker. Distances are measured from the spot of the kick plus 10 yards for the depth of the end zone.

first down – the first play in a set of four downs, or when the offense succeeds in covering 10 yards in the four downs.

fumble – when a player loses possession of the ball before being tackled, normally by contact with an opponent. Either team may recover the ball. The ground cannot cause a fumble.

goal line – the line that divides the end zones from the rest of the field. A touchdown is awarded if the ball breaks the vertical plane of the goal line while in possession or if a receiver catches the ball in the end zone.

huddle – a gathering of the offense or defense to communicate the upcoming play decided by the coach.

interception – a pass caught by a defensive player instead of an offensive receiver. The ball may be returned in the other direction.

lateral – a pass or toss behind the originating player to a teammate as measured by the lines across the field. Although the offense may only make one forward pass per play, there is no limit to the number of laterals at any time.

line of scrimmage – an imaginary line, determined by the ball's location before each play, that extends across the field from sideline to sideline. Seven offensive players must be on the line of scrimmage, though the defense can set up in any formation. Forward passes cannot be thrown from beyond the line of scrimmage.

pass – when the ball is thrown to a receiver who is farther down the field. A team is limited to one such forward pass per play. Normally this is the duty of the quarterback, although technically any eligible receiver can pass the ball.

play action – a type of offensive play in which the quarterback pretends to hand the ball to a running back before passing the ball. The goal is to fool the secondary into weakening their pass coverage.

play clock – visible behind the end zone at either end of the stadium. Once a play is concluded, the offense has 40 seconds to snap the ball for the next play. The duration is reduced to 25 seconds for game-related stoppages such as penalties. Time is kept on the play clock. If the offense does not snap the ball before the play clock elapses, they incur a 5-yard penalty for delay of game.

punt – a kick, taken by a special teams player called the punter, that surrenders possession to the opposing team. This is normally done on fourth down when the offense deems gaining a first down unlikely.

receiver – an offensive player who may legally catch a pass, almost always wide receivers, tight ends, and running backs. Only the two outermost players on either end of the line of scrimmage—even wide receivers who line up distantly from the offensive line—or the four players behind the line of scrimmage (such as running backs, another wide receiver, and the quarterback) are eligible receivers. If an offensive lineman, normally an ineligible receiver, is placed on the outside of the line of scrimmage because of an unusual formation, he is considered eligible but must indicate his eligibility to game officials before the play.

run – a type of offensive play in which the quarterback, after accepting the ball from center, either keeps it and heads upfield or gives the ball to another player, who then attempts to move ahead with the help of blocking teammates.

sack – a play in which the defense tackles the quarterback behind the line of scrimmage on a pass play.

safety – 1) the most uncommon scoring play in football. When an offensive player is tackled in his own end zone, the defensive team is awarded two points and receives the ball via a kick; 2) a defensive secondary position divided into two roles, free safety and strong safety.

snap – the action that begins each play. The center must snap the ball between his legs, usually to the quarterback, who accepts the ball while immediately behind the center or several yards farther back in a formation called the shotgun.

special teams – the personnel that take the field for the punts, kickoffs, and field goals, or a generic term for that part of the game.

tackle – 1) a term for both an offensive and defensive player. The offensive tackles line up on the outside of the line, but inside the tight end, while the defensive tackles protect the interior of their line; 2) the act of forcing a ball carrier to touch the ground with any body part other than the hand or feet. This concludes a play.

tight end – an offensive player who normally lines up on the outside of either offensive tackle. Multiple tight ends are frequently employed on running plays where the offense requires only a modest gain. Roles vary between blocking or running pass routes.

touchdown – scored when the ball breaks the vertical plane of the goal line. Worth six points and the scoring team can add a single additional point by kick or two points by converting from the 2-yard line with an offensive play.

RESOURCES

FURTHER READING

Artell, Mike. *Drew Brees: Football Superstar*. Mankato: Capstone Publishing, 2014.

Challen, Paul. *What Does a Quarterback Do?* New York: The Rosen Publishing Group, Inc., 2015.

Crepeau, Richard C. *NFL Football: A History of America's New National Pastime*. Urbana, Chicago, and Springfield: University of Illinois Press, 2014.

Editors of Sports Illustrated. *Sports Illustrated NFL QB: The Greatest Position in Sports*. New York: Time Home Entertainment, Inc., 2014.

Feldman, Bruce. *The QB: The Making of Modern Quarterbacks*. New York: Three Rivers Press, 2014.

Mack, Larry. *The New Orleans Saints Story*. Hopkins: Bellwether Media, 2016.

Sandler, Michael. *Drew Brees and the New Orleans Saints: Super Bowl XLIV*. New York: Bearport Publishing, 2011.

Wilner, Barry and Ken Rappoport. *On the Clock: The Story of the NFL Draft*. Lanham: Taylor Trade Publishing, 2015.

INTERNET RESOURCES

http://bleacherreport.com/nfl
The official website for Bleacher Report Sport's NFL reports on each of the 32 teams.

https://www.cbssports.com/nfl/teams/page/NO/new-orleans-saints
The web page for the New Orleans Saints provided by CBSSports.com, providing latest news and information, player profiles, scheduling, and standings.

http://www.neworleanssaints.com/
The official website for the New Orleans Saints football club, including history, player information, statistics, and news.

www.espn.com/
The official website of ESPN sports network.

https://www.footballdb.com/teams/nfl/new-orleans-saints/history
The Football Database, a reputable news source, New Orleans Saints web page providing historical rosters, results, statistics, and draft information.

www.nfl.com/
The official website of the National Football League.

www.pro-football-reference.com/
The football specific resource provided by Sports Reference LLC for current and historical statistics of players, teams, scores, and leaders in the NFL, AFL, and AAFC.

https://sports.yahoo.com/nfl/
The official website of Yahoo! Sports NFL coverage, providing news, statistics, and important information about the league and the 32 teams.

INDEX

PHOTO CREDITS

CHAPTER 1

Tech. Sgt. Michael Holzworth via Wikimedia Commons

© Mbr Images | Dreamstime.com

CHAPTER 2

Ian Ransley | Flickr

Redsully | Wikimedia Commons

© Ken Wolter | Dreamstime.com

© Mbr Images | Dreamstime.com

© Jerry Coli | Dreamstime.com

© Jerry Coli | Dreamstime.com

Jeffrey Beall | Wikimedia Commons

CHAPTER 3

Kelly Bailey | Flickr

© Melinda Dove | Dreamstime.com

© Jerry Coli | Dreamstime.com

© Melinda Dove | Dreamstime.com

© Walter Arce | Dreamstime.com

Gudpackage | Wikipedia Commons

CHAPTER 4

Ian Ransley | Flickr

Keith Allison | Wikipedia Commons

© Todd Taulman | Dreamstime.com

© Angie Westre Wieand | Dreamstime.com

© Briannolan | Dreamstime.com

SD Dirk | Wikipedia Commons

CHAPTER 5

Staff Sgt. Beth Del Vecchio via Wikimedia Commons

© Starstock | Dreamstime.com

© Jonathan Weiss | Dreamstime.com

© Calvin L. Leake | Dreamstime.com

© Jonathan Weiss | Dreamstime.com

© Jerry Coli | Dreamstime.com

Sgt. Thomas Day via Wikimedia Commons

EDUCATIONAL VIDEO LINKS

ABOUT THE AUTHOR

Joe L. Morgan is a father, author, and an avid sports fan. He enjoys every type of professional sport, including NFL, NBA, MLB, and European club soccer. He enjoyed a brief career as a punter and a defensive back at the NCAA Division III level, and now spends much of his time watching and writing about the sports he loves.